Work with your dreams
to understand.
Play with your dreams to heal.

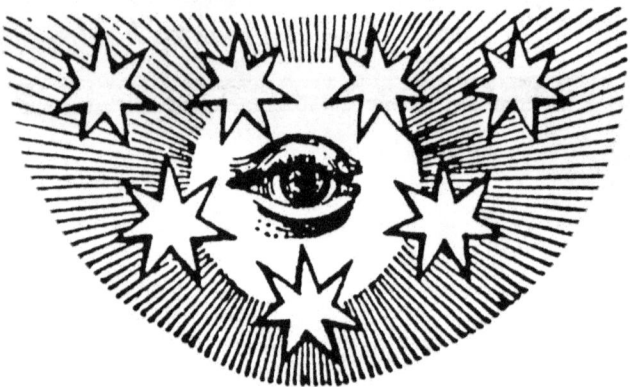

ONEIROGNOSIS
THE ART OF DREAMING

BY

Stephen Barnwell

Antarctica Arts
MMXVIII

A Book From Nadiria,
The Lost Colony of Antarctica

ONEIROGNOSIS

Antarctica Arts
www.AntarcticaArts.com

Hardbound edition
Copyright © 2015 Stephen Barnwell
Paperback edition
Copyright © 2018 Stephen Barnwell

ISBN 978-0-9913216-2-9

ONEIROGNOSIS (oh-nye-ro-NO-sis) stands for Dream Knowledge, from the Greek words Oneiro, which means dream, and Gnosis, meaning knowledge.

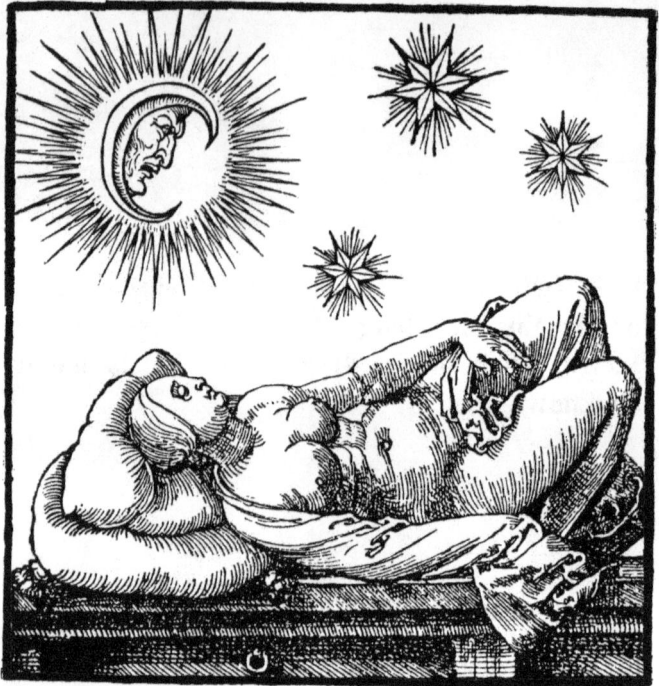

✠

✠

CHAPTER ONE
Where Dreams Happen

DREAMS ARE ENCOUNTERS with a place of being that is starkly alien to our waking lives, yet clothed in its semblance. When we shift our gaze in sleep, a doorway into another reality is suddenly opened. Beyond it is a world just as real as our waking life, yet seen through clouded eyes. Perception is a continuum, like a color spectrum, with ordinary waking life but a single hue.

THE WORLD IN WHICH dreams happen is a dynamic and maleable place, sharing a deep connection with the waking world. People, places, and objects that are important to you have an echo, a reflection in the dreaming world that becomes a vessel for spiritual energy. Once filled, these vessels become living thoughts, children of the Mind. These are the creatures that inhabit our dreams and

speak to us from hidden realms.

IN DREAMS, WE JOURNEY through a strange landscape whose only illumination is the light of the mind. The appearance of strangeness is therefore the result of our need to adapt our vision to the dream world by the understanding of personal symbolism and metaphor. We perceive dream events through the lens of our accreted life experience, encountering

Life-giving rain comes from above, but it collects below. Our waking selves are like the trees of the forest, reaching upwards to the light. Yet just as trees send roots deep below the earth to gather water and nutrients, we also extend our being deep into the spirit world to gather nourishment from our dreams. We are creatures who dwell in two worlds at once; manifest in the material world through our bodies, yet rooted deeply in the firmament of Spirit. As we increase our knowledge of dreams, we strengthen our connection to the Creator.

an unfamiliar world garbed in intimate allegory. Dreams connect us to our deep emotions and memories, creating unifying links between disparate regions of the soul.

OUR TRIUNE NATURE

REFLECTING CREATION, our triune nature is composed of three parts: the Body, the Mind, and the Soul. Dreams act as a bridge connecting these aspects of our selves, helping us to maintain harmony and balance. Our Souls give birth to dreams, which are clothed in icons by our Mind, and they occur only when the

Body rests in sleep. Therefore, dreams are created by all three aspects of our being and inform us not only of ourselves, but also of Creation.

THE FIRST ASPECT of our triune nature is the Body. The body is the physical vehicle which we inhabit while on this earth. It is the material manifestation of ourselves in this world. We are tightly joined to it, but only for a brief time. When we are finished with our bodies, we will discard them, and travel back to the spirit world from whence we came.

THE MIND is the storehouse of all our memories, learning, and experiences. It is our earthly personality, one that we gain through inculturation, socialization, and education. It is the part of ourselves where all of our fears, desires, and knowledge reside. As with the body, the mind is also a temporal aspect of our selves, which shall be stripped away when we travel back to our home in the Spirit.

✳ ✳ ✳

The triune nature of God is mirrored in His Creation: earth, sea, and sky. Likewise, we reflect the Creator with our composition of body, mind, and soul. Everywhere on this earth we see the sacred pattern of triune natures. The essential dynamic of this world, however, is dualism: day and night, male and female, good and evil. Opposing forces combine to produce the third principle, Equilibrium, the secret of nature. Two becomes Three as positive and negative create a null point. Therefore whatever is holy produces balance; whatever is sacred brings peace out of opposition.

THE SOUL IS THE ONLY permanent aspect of our selves. It is our true self, unfettered by childish fears and material yearnings. This is why children raised by the same parents in the same environment may grow to be such different

personalties. Our souls are unique and pre-existent of our incarnation in this world. It is our souls that best mirror the Creator, for we are but emanations of the Eternal Spirit.

DREAMS ARE THE VOICE of the soul, clothed in intimate symbolism by the mind. The purity of the soul's voice is what enchants us; it is what gives dreams their essence of nourishment and mystery.

We enter the spiritual countryside of dreams only through our souls, but the experience is filtered through the mind, and that is where obfuscation is introduced.

THE MIND CLUTTERS DREAMS with allegory and symbolism, confusing the encounter with remnants of our memories, wrapping the pure essence of the spiritual with familiar and comprehensible metaphor. This is why dreamwork is a twofold endeavor: we must cherish the manifest dream as a valuable experience, but we also must unwrap the gift to see the spiritual beneath the mundane. This is the Great Work, for to understand our dreams is to come into contact with our very souls.

Dreams, Children of the Soul, are born naked and pure. They are clothed by the Mind in their many forms and semblances.

YOUR INNER LANGUAGE

WHEN WE WALK the dream landscape, we experience life using a highly symbolic language. It is as if we are encountering things so outside of our senses that our minds are forced to create similes or metaphors to give shape to what we are experiencing. In our dreamwork, we find that the more we remember and attempt to understand our dreams, the greater our awareness of our symbolic patterns becomes. It is as if we are deaf and dumb, isolated and disconnected in a strange and unseen world. We caress the strange shapes around us,

---

As from a great distance, the Soul sings to us in songs of yearning. Its voice echoes down the convoluted halls of memory, pulsing to the rhythm of our Mind, transforming into the Psalm of the Spirit.

---

trying to imagine our surroundings. Through careful attention to our dreams, however, we may learn to see and hear in a new way, unlocking the intimate secrets of our deepest selves.

THERE IS NO SET "dream language" that we must memorize; there is only the learning to recognize the patterns and symbols unique to ourselves. Our minds do not store memories in a literal fashion, but translate our experiences into symbols, or what are called Artifacts. These Artifacts represent the distillation of a memory, the solidifying of a thought into an iconic shape. An Artifact may be anything: a person, an object, or a place. Each of us has an individual way of seeing and remembering the world, using unique metaphors to embody the essence of experience. No one else can tell you what your dream symbols mean. That is for you alone to discover.

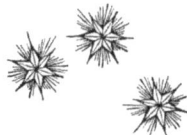

CAREFUL DREAMWORK, through recollection, journaling, and meditation, will yield a pattern between waking events and dream metaphors. It is the work of the dreamer to associate events in your waking life with the events in your dreams to deduce a connection, and to see how your inner mind uses symbols to express itself.

DREAMS AND TIME

DREAMS EXIST OUTSIDE of our normal waking time. We may dream of things that have happened, are happening now, or may happen in the future. Although seeding dreams of the future is not possible, we may catch accidental glimpses of events that may yet come to be. We all have had moments when we feel that we have been in a circumstance before, talked to a person we only just met, or perhaps feel that we have been to a place we have never visited previously. This experience of things Already Seen, or "deja vu", occurs when we have dreamt of an event, place, or person before we actually live it in waking life. A forgotten dream is never truly forgotten, but memory may be triggered by encountering dreamt-of events. This is why recording dreams in journals may provide confirmation of previously dreamed events if such a sensation is observed.

DREAMS OF THE FUTURE are rare and unpredictable. Yet while their numbers are few, most cannot possibly come to pass because of the choices we make. The future of our lives is not yet written, laying out a wide field of possibilities before us. Each choice we make limits that field, until only a narrow path remains. Dreams may sometimes see what lies ahead down one of life's many paths, either chosen or unchosen.

The great Wheel of Time turns unceasingly, grinding the mundane world to dust under its unyielding tread. As we dream, we travel along the spokes of that Wheel approaching the still point at the center, which is the Creator. The dreamer is the one who escapes time, who apprehends eternity.

YOUR DREAM HOUSE

OF ALL PLACES THAT EXIST in your dream world, there is one special place that is the metaphor for your soul. This is called your Dream House, where your memories, desires, secrets, fears, and wishes reside.

IN YOUR DREAM HOUSE is stored each sensation of your life, every thought, word, and deed, transmuted into symbols that represent the shape of your daily encounters. It is growing every day, like a crystal forming around your soul, reflecting all your life's experiences. Many times your Dream House takes the form of an actual house you lived in, usually the house you grew up in as a child. This is because you started to gather memories at birth and needed a place to store them. The house you explored as a child provided the only structure you knew, and was thus employed to provide a framework for referencing

memory. What was external was made
internal. However, any familiar location that you repeatedly return to in
your dreams may be your Dream House.

THE SIZE OF YOUR DREAM
house grows each day, and the
contents of its rooms interact,
change, and grow over time. By careful
exploration and mapping of your Dream
House, you may chart the interplay of
the Artifacts and draw conclusions

from them. Remember that an **Artifact** may be anyone or anything; a person, place, or object. New experiences may be accreted onto existing **Artifacts**, rather than forming new ones. This changes the appearance and influence of these **Artifacts**. Meticulous study of our dreams may help us to notice these changes and to understand their implications.

We build our House with every sight we see, every sound we hear, every thought we conceive. Like a vast mansion which grows larger with time, the mind adds room after room of experiences as life progresses. Our nocturnal self wanders the endless corridors of our Dream House, exploring the crowded rooms filled to overflowing with the very stuff of life: Artifacts of consciousness preserved in the amber of sleep.

YOUR DREAM HOUSE is continually expanding, adding new rooms in which to store the ceaseless influx of experience, thought, and memory. As in a physical dwelling, your Dream House organizes its many rooms on a variety of floors. It may be ventured that the levels in your House represent the various strata of your mind. For many, the lower levels contain Artifacts of your emotions, or the unconscious, primal self. The main floors contain the Artifacts of daily life, while the attic might reflect the loftier constructs of your higher self, or plans for the future. Those who have ventured onto the roof of their Dream House have discovered connections to the universe or the spirit world. It is a veritable museum of Artifacts, all crowded into thematically organized rooms. The job of the dreamer is to explore the Dream House, drawing detailed maps and cataloging its contents.

In your House, the museum of the Mind, memories and dreams dance together. Playfully, they exchange gifts and trade masks, as if at a grand ball. From their union, new Artifacts are born. These children are living things, like their parents, who change and grow with Time.

DREAM SEEDING

MOST DREAMS are experienced passively, like watching a play upon a stage. You can, however, have dreams that respond to your attention. Dreams are living experiences, a connection to a more spiritual plane, and we may ask our dreams questions and expect an answer. The process of self-interrogation and having dreams in response to it is called Dream Seeding.

QUESTIONS MAY BE POSED to our deepest selves to discover how we truly feel about something, or to gain access to memories hidden beneath the veil of forgetfulness. We may ask our bodies about our ailments, or use our minds to solve problems as we sleep. Our dreams are responsive to our needs and are a treasure trove of wisdom and knowledge waiting to be unearthed.

THERE IS NO MAGIC in Dream Seeding, neither is it a method for fortune-telling. Dream Seeding is merely a tool to concentrate on the Question being posed, a device that focuses the mind and tunes the

Dreams will never be your servants; they cannot be summoned, coerced, or compelled. Dreams might be lured, however. They may be invited or even coaxed to embrace you. Dream Seeding is a seductive dance between the waking mind and the inner spirit.

spirit. It is a tool for discovering the inner mind's secrets, for recovering memories, and listening directly to the heart without the clutter and distraction of waking life.

THE PROCESS OF SEEDING your dreams involves forming a question that is answerable by your inner mind. Seeking answers for events of which you have no knowledge, or about the future, is not possible.

Dreams may reliably draw upon our personal reservoir of experience, knowledge, skills, and emotions. Self-knowledge is the goal of all enlightenment, and dream seeding is a powerful mechanism to achieve this.

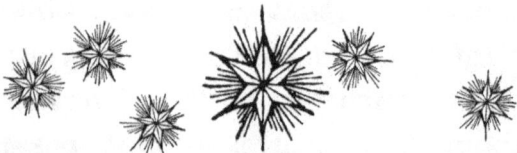

We gaze intently into the dark pool of our dreams. What returns our gaze are the wavering reflections of ourselves, yearning to be seen. For Desire is the heart of dreaming. Our deepest self seeks love and attention from our waking self. Neglect of dreams is the death of the Soul, while the love and nurturing of them gives the Soul life.

✠

CHAPTER TWO

Types of Dreams

WHILE THE SPECTRUM of dreams is wide and diverse, there are only seven principle types. The kinds of dreams that respond well to seeding fall into five main categories: Healing Dreams, Decision Dreams, Puzzle Dreams, Exploratory Dreams, and Sister Dreams. The other types, Visitation Dreams and Waking Dreams, are experiences of a different order, less responsive to seeding or any other form of guidance.

SOME EXPERIENCES in waking life have significance, while others do not. So it is in dreams, where some dreams have significance or meaning while others do not. Dream seeding teaches us to guide our dreams and make use of them, creating purposeful activities rather than random recreation. Remember, however, that all work must be balanced with play.

Keep a balance in your dreamwork between active dream seeding and passive enjoyment of your dream gifts.

HEALING DREAMS

HEALING DREAMS PROVIDE healing to the dreamer, whether it be for mind, body, or spirit. When there is disease, it is best to discover the root cause of the ailment in order to embark on a course of treatment. Often, however, the causes of our maladies are unknown or hidden from our conscious mind. Healing Dreams may reveal the source of physical illness as well as emotional, mental, or spiritual affliction.

OUR BODIES SPEAK TO US constantly, but we are often ignorant of their language. Dreaming is one of several languages our bodies use to communicate with

The Garden of our Dreams contains a strange and wonderful variety of species. Like flowers, some dreams are pleasing to the senses; Like fruit, other dreams are nourishing and wholesome food; Like thorns, some dreams are painful and serve as warnings; Like trees, some dreams may last a lifetime and serve as landmarks, guiding our way.

our conscious mind. By asking the deeper self to show us the causes of the disorder, our waking selves may gain the knowledge needed to heal an ailing body.

BESIDES THE SIMPLE gathering of information, Healing Dreams may also act as agents of healing energy. By accepting the manifest imagery in a dream as reality, we may be able to apply healing force directly to the body or mind. In a dream, if your hand is on fire, douse it with water; if you are covered with parasites, remove them; if your house is infested with vermin, eradicate them. Whatever form disease may take in your dreams, positive and responsible actions in the dreaming world have direct consequence in the waking world.

FEAR, ANGER, OR SHAME is often the largest obstacle that must be overcome in order to achieve healing. Some emotional memories are so ancient as to be completely forgotten by our waking selves, yet nothing is hidden from the dreaming self. In

Healing Dreams we may explore our Dream House to find the source of the harmful emotions, exposing them to the light of consciousness, and healing them through forgiveness and acceptance.

HEALING DREAMS MAY ALSO be seeded for other persons beside the dreamer himself. It is best to know intimately the person for whom you are seeding a Healing Dream, but it is not necessary.

All of Creation shares an essential spiritual connection; thus Healing Dreams for others may be fruitful since dreams have their origins in the realm of the spirit. The spiritual connection we all share links us more directly and profoundly in our dreams, allowing us to channel God's healing energy more efficiently.

THE SEEDING OF a Healing Dream is an act that sends healing energy either inward towards yourself, or outward towards another. Dreams have the mysterious property to nurture the soul, and the focusing of the mind on the process of healing transforms the self into an agent of healing force. The Creator of all things is the source of life and healing, and we all may be conduits of His life-giving emanations. Thus it is possible that our very dreams themselves may cure us of our maladies and afflictions.

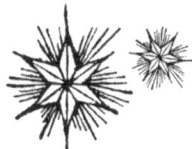

DECISION DREAMS

LIFE IS AN ENDLESS PARADE of choices that we all must endure. Decision Dreams enable us to make difficult choices by tapping into our deepest memory, emotion, and intellect. We all have a vast reservoir of memories that are not always accessible to our waking mind. In Decision Dreams we wander through our Dream House and examine all of our stored knowledge and experience. This accumulated wisdom helps us to understand the larger forces that may be involved in our decision, as well as to remember all the facts and details that we may have acquired regarding a particular situation.

DECISION DREAMS also allow our deeper emotions to have their say in making a choice. How we really feel about this decision may have an important impact, without the rationalizations, excuses, and other intellectual obfuscations that often cloud the issue. Our true feelings are often disguised or suppressed under conscious mandates, no matter how well-intentioned. These emotions, even if they are unreasonable or childish, are worthy of study and reflection. Inner discord is frequently avoided simply by being aware of all the conflicting forces within us.

THE DECISIONS WE MAKE do not exist in a vacuum. There are many exterior forces at work that may have an impact on the outcome of our choices. Decision Dreams help us to see the bigger picture, to get a bird's eye view of the landscape of our situation. All living things are interconnected, and dreams are but one place where all things share a common consciousness, a united place

of being. Greater understanding of
the diverse and subtle connections between all things increases the wisdom
of our decisions.

ONCE AGAIN, POSITIVE ACTION
in your dreams is strongly
encouraged. When faced with a
difficult choice in a dream, overcome
your fears and take the darker path.
That which is hidden must be exposed
to the light. Doors must be unlocked;
obstacles must be overcome. The

stones we remove from our paths clear the way for our souls to continue our journey.

As we learn from our dreams, we build bridges within our divided Self, healing our fractured Soul. All of us are broken in some way, and self-knowledge through our dreams is a wholesome and healing force.

PUZZLE DREAMS

A S WE NAVIGATE THE endless labyrinth of life, our dreams help us utilize hidden memories, skills, and resources to find our way. Puzzle Dreams help us to solve problems, find lost objects, or receive artistic inspiration.

W E USE OUR ANALYTICAL minds together with intuition, emotions, and memory to fit the pieces of a puzzle together. Solving

*The dreaming mind is capable of
untangling the knots
that the waking mind has tied.*

problems is often a creative endeavor, and our dreams give us a deep connection to our creativity. Puzzle Dreams tap into hidden reserves of intuition so that we may approach problems from a new perspective.

DAY TO DAY DISTRACTIONS often interfere with the mind's ability to concentrate and solve problems, but dreams have no such limitations. Unfettered by the clutter of daily living, dreams examine the world with a unique clarity of vision; a stronger, more penetrating gaze.

ONE PRACTICAL USE of Puzzle Dreams is to help find lost objects. Memories of insignificant events are accessible only through dreams, because the conscious mind has insufficient resources to handle such an immense amount of information. While every sensation we experience is recorded by our minds, the bulk of it finds its way to our Dream House, locked away from our waking selves. Through Puzzle Dreams, we can examine the contents of our House and find what was misplaced, discarded, stored, or lost. We mount nocturnal expeditions of discovery, and what we find will always be rewarding.

PLACED IN THE CATEGORY of Puzzle Dreams is the seeking of artistic inspiration or the removal of an artistic blockage. With our dreams we may penetrate the barrier between the physical world and the spiritual world, reaching the realm of the Creator, source of all inspiration. Our deepest reserves of creativity are in the spiritual world, and Puzzle Dreams are able to tap that reservoir. If the wellspring is blocked, however, we may dream a way to remove the stones and clear the well, so that we may dip our buckets once again. As above, so below; what is

---

A decision is a balance, an agreement, a truce made between the Mind and the Heart. As Nature always seeks balance, so we, too, must strive for equilibrium in all things. Inner peace is the foundation of our entire House; likewise, inner discord undermines all things.

---

restored in our dreams is restored in our waking lives.

EXPLORATORY DREAMS

WHILE OTHER TYPES of dreams may serve practical purposes in the world, Exploratory Dreams inspire us to be anthropologists, digging through the relics of our past. As we pass through life's transformations, our spirits are continually reborn, sloughing off husks of memories as a snake sheds its skin. In dreams, we find ourselves surrounded by the discarded or hidden constructions of our minds. Exploratory Dreams take us on expeditions of self-discovery, returning with trophies of truth and knowledge.

LITTLE PRACTICAL ADVICE may be given regarding Exploratory Dreams as the environs you explore are uniquely your own. Discovering and mapping your Dream House is an excellent purpose for

Exploratory Dreams. As stated above,
the appearance of your Dream House
may not be obvious, but its identi-
fication and examination are crucial to
your development as a dreamworker.

YOU WILL DISCOVER that the
majority of the important breakthroughs and epiphanies in
your life are enshrined in your Dream
House. Thus, it is expected that many
of your dreamwork breakthroughs will
occur in your Dream House as well. A

catalogue of its **Artifacts** and denizens will serve as a useful reference in learning your inner language.

THE TECHNIQUE OF dream seeding may assist you in many things, one of which is the ability to return to places or discourse with people that were dreamt of previously. Individual dreams are often puzzling and obscure, yet repeated dreams of the same subject provide a wealth of material for further meditation. Fruitful dream-work often involves returning to the same theme over a period of time in order to examine the situation from a variety of perspectives.

EACH DREAM PROVIDES a piece of the puzzle so that a more complete picture may be assembled, yielding an answer to our Question. Receiving an answer is assured; understanding what the answer is telling us requires wisdom and experience.

SISTER DREAMS

TIME HAS NO POWER over dreams. Groups or series of dreams may occur over a period of weeks, months, or even years. The previous night's dream may have a direct relation to a dream experienced over a decade ago, as well as to a dream that will not arrive for many years to come. Sister dreams are interlocking pieces of the same puzzle. When viewed together, they yield a clearer picture of our inner life.

WHAT LINKS SISTER dreams together may come from a variety of sources. They may be expressions of a strong emotion struggling to be recognized by the waking mind, eager for fulfilment, forgiveness, or healing. The dreams may be attempts to solve a long-standing problem or issue that needs resolution. Perhaps your body is suffering from a disease and is trying to warn you or provide a path to healing. There

could essentially be any reason why your soul is attempting to communicate a message or bring to the attention of the waking mind an issue of importance.

RECOGNIZING SISTER DREAMS is a crucial ability that must be achieved over time. This is why keeping, and frequently reviewing, a dream journal is essential. Over the course of time you may recognize recurring themes, characters, objects, behavior, colors, foods, places, music, or words. Virtually any repeated **Artifact** or event may signal the presence of **Sister Dreams**. Patience and intuition are required to identify patterns and linkages between disparate dream experiences. This ability will increase with diligent effort, as you become more skillful in your dreamwork.

Dreams are Children of the Soul. Some dreams are solitary children, while others are orphans. Yet many have sisters, daughters of a proflegate and potent Mother.

THE REWARDS OF identifying and meditating on Sister Dreams are great. One could argue that all your dreams are sisters, as your path to self-discovery is a continuum of growth. True Sister Dreams, however, have much closer relation to each other and therefore reflect a stronger impulse and a more potent generative motivation. Whatever is giving birth to these Sisters is obviously stronger and more urgent than that of other dreams, and when brought into waking perception will yield proportionally more powerful fruit.

VISITATION DREAMS

WHEN OUR CREATOR reaches out and speaks to us directly, these are Visitation Dreams. These dreams are rare events, and happen only on special occasions, and only when needed. Our daily lives so distract and blind us to God's presence that we are deaf to His still, small voice in our soul. Yet the more we probe and familiarize ourselves with the realm of the spirit, the more we attune ourselves to the song of the Creator.

MOST DREAMS ARE generated by our soul, resonating from deep within. Visitation Dreams come from outside ourselves. They

are intrusions from a spiritual reality
separate from our own being. The
hallmark of a Visitation is the over-
whelming sensation of power and
love. The form the Visitor will take
may be human or an appearance
unknown to our experience, but it will
always be specific and personified
in some way. Further, the Visitor will
always be loving or protective; there
is no darkness in the Creator.

WHAT HAPPENS IN a Visitation is normally the impartation of wisdom. If you are confronted by a powerful, wise being, it is permissible to seek knowledge. Ask what questions you may; be sincere and do not be afraid. Our task in life is to grow in love. True wisdom, then, is knowledge governed by love.

A VISITATION DREAM is one of the greatest gifts you will ever receive. While normal dreams are gifts from your deeper self, a Visitation is a wondrous gift from

In the fury of an electrical storm, lightning may strike miles apart, but still be from the same storm. Likewise, Sister Dreams may be separated by a span of years, but are still products of a single emotional tempest raging across the seasons and landscapes of the soul.

your Creator. It is an emanation from the source of light and love, shining directly into your heart. These dreams are always remembered, usually lucid, and should be treasured for a lifetime.

The walls we build to silence the voice of the Creator are destroyed in dreams. God is always seeking to speak with us, yet we often refuse to hear. In our dreams, God may speak to us directly. Listen for His voice.

WAKING DREAMS

THE MOST IMPORTANT TYPE of dream, one which does not respond to dream seeding, is called a Waking or Lucid Dream. This kind of dream represents a higher level of dreaming, a state of consciousness above normal experience. Waking Dreams occur when you realize that you are dreaming while you are within the dream. This knowledge releases your Mind to wander freely off the prescribed path and make conscious actions.

AWAKE WITHIN SLEEP, we see the fiber of reality first-hand. This is the highest form of dreaming, a skill that is greatly sought-for. By practice and sustained effort, we may achieve this state of awareness, and constant work must be done to retain this elusive ability.

LEARNING THE SKILL to achieve Waking Dreams is a difficult endeavor. Dream seeding can be helpful in this process, but you must ask for a Waking Dream each night, rather than asking a Question. You should simply affirm that you will be awake and aware in your dreams that night.

THE WAKING DREAM is extremely fragile and doubt can threaten its stability, which is why confidence in your belief in the dreaming state is important. The lucid state can also be quickly ended by strong emotion, so it is best to remain calm while experiencing the Waking Dream state. Concentration and assurance are key.

A SURE SIGNPOST of the Waking Dream is the False Awakening, which is a dream where we are convinced that we have awakened, but are in reality still dreaming. False Awakenings are daughters of Waking Dreams, for one naturally gives birth to the other. A False Awakening may lead to a Waking Dream, or it may be a product of a previous one.

As Faith can move mountains, so expectations determine the shape of your dreams. Wandering in the darkness of sleep, the light of our souls attracts dreams as moths to a flame. Fear amplifies fear, while Joy increases joy. By force of will, we may pierce the veil of self-deception and shape the essence of the spirit into the desires of the mind.

O **AWAKEN WITHIN** your dreams is to explore the frontier between the material world and the realm of the spirit with open eyes and a clear mind. The scales fall from our eyes and we see beyond the veil of self-deception, revealing the truth of our being and the ground on which it stands. True, purposeful action will be gained, and with it will come deep knowledge of ourselves and the world of the spirit.

Believe that something will happen in your dreams and it will be so, if your belief is absolute. For in our dreams, we do not doubt our surroundings, we believe in their reality. But if we dare to question that reality, then we may see through the illusion, and percieve the dream-world as it truly is. Awakening inside your dreams requires a willingness to abandon your senses and logic and take a leap of faith. Then, with confidence and assurance, we may gain mastery of our dream-world, and make all our desires a reality.

Have Faith in your dreams.

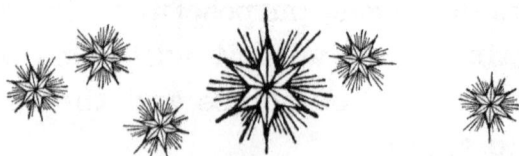

✠

CHAPTER THREE

Your Dream Research

IN ORDER TO SEED YOUR dreams, you must first ask yourself a Question. The Question may be about any aspect of your physical, emotional, or spiritual life. The Question may include all of your family, friends, associates, and acquaintances as well. Self-interrogation usually begins with questions regarding our daily lives, but as dreams come in response to them, deeper and more probing questions must follow our answers. In dreams, we tell ourselves many stories, our Souls teaching our Minds through parables.

WHEN SPECIFIC and potent metaphors are presented in our dreams, it is prudent to alter our questioning to explore more fully the implications of those metaphors. For we must penetrate many veils of symbolism to arrive at the Truth of

the dream. Be not afraid to follow the trail exposed by your dreams, for in doing so, you enter into a dialog with your soul.

DREAMS USE THE LANGUAGE of symbolic imagery and metaphor, and the way we ask a question determines the content of our dream responses. Translating the Question into the dream's own language enables us to interrogate our dreams directly, rather than obliquely. By working with manifest dream imagery, that is by addressing the symbols and events in our dreams as genuine, living experiences, we may more fruitfully decipher the secrets of our inner language. When a door is locked in your dreams, it is better to find a key than to speculate on what the door may represent. As you come to a well, drink from its water. If you come to a river, swim in it and let the current carry you wherever it may.

ASKING THE QUESTION

N GENERAL, THERE ARE two ways to seed your dreams: through a form of self-hypnosis, and through prayer. Both methods are fruitful, depending on your goals, mood, and relationship with God.

HE MOST COMMON METHOD of self-interrogation is to decide on a question, and then repeat the question over and over until the point of sleep. Mental discipline is required because as you approach the gateway of sleep, your mind increasingly wanders. Also, when you are on the verge of sleep you will have "pre-dreams" or hypnogogic imagery. These are not true dreams, but merely the conscious mind letting go of control and releasing unused energy. Try to regain control and focus on your question for as long as possible. Form a visual image of the Question as well as a verbal query, because this will help block out competing voices and thoughts that will distract you. Picture in your mind the place you want to go, the person you wish to speak with, or the object you are looking for until sleep overtakes you.

IF YOU HAVE A RELATIONSHIP with God, it is better to ask Him for help and guidance with your dreams. Our Creator knows us better than we know ourselves, and will always assist us in gaining knowledge and wisdom. Trusting in the inherent goodness of the Creator, we may seek His help and ask God for dreams

of wisdom and clarity. Arrogance is
the path to darkness, while humility
is the road to enlightenment. Acknow-
ledging our smallness in the face
of Creation, and placing the will of
God before our own, brings us into
harmony with all things.

COMBINATION OF meditation
and prayer is very effective.
You may also write the Question
onto a slip of paper, or draw a picture

of your dream destination or the object of inquiry, and put it under your pillow. Use whatever method you are most comfortable with to keep your mind focused on the Question until the point of sleep.

FORMING A DIALOGUE

THE ESSENCE OF DREAM seeding is asking the proper questions. When seeking answers or inspiration, it is best to start with a general question, such as "Where did

All of Creation yearns to teach us wisdom if we but ask it. The plants, the winds, the sea, and the stars all instruct us in the patterns and cycles of Creation. Knowledge does not come unbidden, however; it must be sought. Ask your Questions with forethought and care, for the answers will reflect the sincerity of the interrogator.

I put my mother's ring?" or "Should I go to Maine this summer?" or "What is my next novel about?" Broad and general questions are the best way to begin a dialogue with your inner self, but you must be responsive in your conversation. You will undoubtedly receive a dream in answer to your question, but most likely it will not be an obvious answer. It may not even seem like an answer at all. This is when you must probe more deeply.

OUR DREAMS WILL respond to your interrogations with oblique and symbolic answers. It is unfruitful to keep asking the same question night after night. If you ask about a decision, but have a dream about an abandoned barn in a field, ask yourself, "What is in that barn?" Accept the manifest dream imagery and be thankful for it. Then explore more deeply.

Y CONTINUING YOUR dialogue with your dreams and accepting the symbolic imagery in them, you are taking your dreams by the hand

Like a child, play with your dreams. A child does not analyze or study, but accepts and loves. Embrace your dreams and dance with them. They are a part of your Soul that wants to engage with your Mind, but uses a language that the Mind has forgotten. The language of the Soul is the vocabulary of emotion, and dreams are emotions wrapped in the symbolism of memory and allegory.

and starting to dance. At times you should lead the dance, at other times you should relinquish control. As if peeling back the layers of an onion, explore the symbols in your dreams: open the closed doors, feed the hungry animal, light the unlit candle, fix the broken object. Your verbal inquiry is only the crude beginning of a far more subtle and obscure exchange.

WORKING WITH ARTIFACTS

THE PERSONS, PLACES, AND things in your dreams are called Artifacts. As with archeological artifacts, dream artifacts are remnants, traces, and clues which help us discover and understand the deeper mysteries buried in our souls. The essence of dream seeding is how you work with your Artifacts, symbols which point to greater meaning. You must accept them as real and true, understanding that your manipulation of them has consequences in the waking world. Rather than analyzing and dissecting your Artifacts, which is the application of the mind, you should embrace them, which is the employment of the heart. As you interact with your Artifacts over time, you will learn your inner vocabulary so that you may have a true dialogue with your dreams.

IN WAKING DREAMS, when you are aware that you are dreaming, you may interact with your Artifacts directly. Confront and interrogate your Artifacts with clarity of mind and forethought, but always with love and compassion. You may seed your dreams with the intention of meeting a particular person or exploring a specific location. With Waking Dreams, you may establish and maintain a long-term relationship with any person in the dreamtime. Your conversations will be deeply fruitful and enlightening, because you are talking directly to your own soul.

MOST COMMONLY, you will interact with your Artifacts over time through a series of Sister Dreams. One question will lead to another as your dream seeding follows the path illumined by your experiences. Follow those paths wherever they may lead. As you encounter new and potent Artifacts, seed new dreams to explore them further. Weeks or months may be required to fully explore one question, and then you must probe deeper with new questions, exploring the Artifacts fully.

DEDICATION IS REQUIRED

MAINTAINING A COURSE of dream study is a serious endeavor; dedication, work, and commitment are necessary for the long-term success of your inner exploration. Dreamwork is a physical effort as much as a mental effort, for it is at a time when we are most fatigued that work is required of us. The rewards for this hard work are abundant and rich: an active and responsive dream life creates a true sense of satisfaction and well-being, enriching our waking life and bringing peace of mind. This peace comes from the increased balance between our dreaming and waking selves; as internal communication reduces conflict and tension, so dream awareness creates inner harmony.

Each and every dream we are given is but a small piece of a grand and lovely puzzle. As we painstakingly fit the pieces together over a lifetime of dreaming, a flawed and imperfect image of our soul slowly emerges.

IT HAS BEEN DEMONSTRATED that dreams occur with varying frequency in different phases of the night. It appears that dreams occur more often as morning approaches, with an increase in both frequency and duration. The later we sleep in the morning, the better dreams we will experience, and often an afternoon nap will yield powerful dreams, increased recall, and cogent states of consciousness.

SLEEP FIRST ATTENDS to the healing and restoration of the body, and only afterwards does it nurture and grow the mind through dreams. Aided with this knowledge, you may more effectively establish a sleep pattern most enabling for dreaming.

IT IS BEST TO WAKE naturally, without any external element waking you at a set time. Always keep a notebook and a pen at the bedside, for dreams must be recorded as quickly as possible after waking. Do not wait until morning to record the dream, it must be done immediately if waking occurs during the night. Be sure to record anything, even a single word, thought, name, or event. Any miniscule fragment of a dream is worth saving and preserving in order to increase dream awareness and break through the barriers of forgetfulness.

UPON AWAKENING from a dream, it is best to remain in the same position as when dreaming: do not move, do not sit up, do not open your eyes. Simply lie there and review the dream several times. Only after that should you open your eyes and sit up. For any change will flood your mind with sensation and thought, driving away the fragile and delicate memories of the dream.

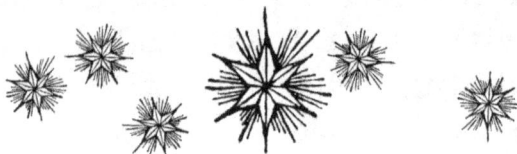

Dreams are Gifts which must be treasured. To cherish these gifts, we adopt an aspect of gratitude and humility as we accept blessings from the Giver of all good things,

TENDING THE DREAM TREE

LIFE IS LIKE A GARDEN filled with growing things - those that are natural and inherent to our being, and those that we have planted ourselves. The trees in our garden may include our marriage, children, friendships, home, business, art, health, and dreams. They are living things that grow with time, and need tending and care to grow properly.

ALL THE TREES IN YOUR garden are tended in different ways, each according to its nature. If neglected, they may wither and die. The Dream Tree is tended by four primary tasks: journaling, meditation, sharing, and manifesting.

THE MOST BASIC dreamwork tool is the journal. A journal must be kept of every single dream, along with the date and time of the dream, plus any important events that are occurring in your waking life. By recording the events in your waking life alongside your dreams, a correlation may be established which will aid in the understanding of your inner language. All fragments of dreams must be faithfully transcribed, no matter how small or trivial. Every sight, sound, word, or emotion is worthy of documentation and study.

DREAMS ARE LIVING THINGS that respond to attention. The best way to increase your ability to dream is to invest more time and attention in the dreams you are now having. Detailing the occurrences of sickness is especially useful, as the body gives us ample warning signs of impending illness, especially in our dreams.

KEEPING A JOURNAL is also important in detecting long-term patterns of dream events. The people, places, and objects in your dreams change over time, evolving and growing just as you do. You may look back on a dream after many years and come to an entirely different understanding of that dream because of the changes and perspective of time. Observing how your dreams change over the years, and are linked together

as Sisters, creates a map of your soul's journey, yielding insight to help navigate the future.

MEDITATION UPON YOUR dreams is essential for proper dream study. Time must be spent in a quiet place meditating upon the dream at hand. Care must be taken to immerse the mind as fully as possible in the memory of the dream, remembering any sights, sounds, smells, or feelings from the dream experience. Fragments of dreams may thus be used to recover complete dreams. Nightmares may be examined and fears confronted. If a dream cannot be recalled, it is often best to remember the end of a dream, and work your way backwards to arrive at the beginning. In this way, you may examine all aspects of your dream; no detail is unimportant. Be sure to record all your new recollections, as well as any emotional reaction to their remembrance. The emotions of the dream hold the key to understanding the dream; let your emotions be your guide in perceiving the relevance and truth of the events in the dream.

SHARING YOUR DREAMS is another path to understanding your dreams. By telling a dream to others, we are forced to verbalize the events and symbols of the dream. The act of speaking brings the dream into the material world in a way that makes us confront the dream in a worldly environment. Our emotional reaction to sharing dreams with others may provide clues to where the emotional heart of the dream lies. Telling your dreams to a trusted friend or fellow dreamworker will help with both recollection and understanding. Many times, the outside perspective of others may give new insight or reveal new patterns in our dreams. Dreamtelling is always a fruitful and enjoyable endeavor.

MANIFESTING YOUR dreams is a method of reconnecting with the moments in your dreams where actions or rituals were performed. If you ate a certain food in your

To meditate on your dreams is to hold a flower cupped in your hands. Care and gentleness allow the memory of the dream to live, and in so living it may yet continue to grow and blossom as time goes by. Water your dreams with love and attention and your life will be enriched with beauty.

dream, be sure to eat that food in the same way, meditating on the dream as you do so. If you performed an act, such as riding a bicycle, go out and ride your bicycle in the same or similar place as in the dream - again, remembering the dream as you are doing so. Be sure to record any new memories of the dream if they occur during this process. If you sang a song in the dream, it is good for you to sing

the same song upon waking, or in a period of meditation where dream memories are being summoned. This technique of Manifesting is helpful in placing the waking mind in the environs of the dreamworld, to create a sense of being inside the dream while awake. This aids in memory as well as deepening the dream awareness for increased dreaming in the future.

AS IN ALL CREATION, dreams have their own natural rhythms and cycles. Your Dream Tree has seasons of bearing fruit and lying fallow, of growing and being pruned, of blossoming and withering. As living things, your dreams have a variety of cycles: daily, monthly, yearly, and even longer. Patience and observation are required to understand your natural inner cycles.

AS YOUR DREAM TREE grows, its fruit will subtly change over time. Be mindful of the changes your symbology will naturally undergo as time progresses. The Artifacts in

The Seasons of your Soul are reflected in your dreams. Patience and dedication will surely bear fruit.

your Dream House will transform due to interaction with other Artifacts in your House. The landmarks of your dream landscape constantly shift, evolve, and grow, autonomously rearranging themselves in a continual nocturnal dance. Memories engage in relationships with each other, sharing and learning from their interaction. Self-knowledge remains hidden to the waking mind until discovered in your dreams, and then brought into the light of understanding.

WHAT YOUR DREAMS MEAN

DREAMS ARE ESSENTIALLY normal human experiences, and should be considered as such. To dismiss them as frivolous, meaning-

less, or unreal strips dreams of their potential for enriching your life. Dreams should always live in your memory as vivid and potent experiences, alongside all the other important memories you treasure. To interpret a dream, that is to assign it a fixed and simple meaning, is to kill that dream. Like a butterfly pinned to an archival board, the "interpreted" dream is a beautiful, yet ultimately dead thing.

Therefore allow your dreams to possess all the complexity and reality that your other memories have. Enjoy the manifest dream as a literal act, to cherish as an achievement that strengthens the soul.

I T ALSO MUST BE impressed upon the reader that dreams are not "messages" from anything external, except for those rare dreams given to us by the Creator in Visitation Dreams. Most dreams are experiences in a more spiritual world, a reality somewhat more profound than our ordinary waking lives. The dreaming mind clothes these experiences in the garments of your life, giving your dreams potency and mysticism.

T HESE EXPLORATIONS of the spiritual world are wrapped in a cloth woven from your memories, emotions, and desires. Dreams are not fabricated images or stories authored by some unseen hand, static creations to which we must assign only one meaning, but are dynamic, living events in our lives. They are events that must be given the same importance given to all other experiences in our lives to become truly meaningful.

EACH PERSON HAS A different inner language, and symbols appearing in your dreams have unique meanings known only to you. While there may be some common metaphors that seem universal in consequence, most encounters you will have in the dream world are seen through your own inner vision, and recorded using your own personal filing system for memories, which are the Artifacts.

UNDERSTANDING YOUR dreams will come through meditation and careful study. Common sense and your intuition will guide you in the understanding of your symbology, but keep in mind that symbols may relate to concepts or memories in unexpected ways. Humor and puns are common in dreams, reminding us that dreams are frequently a source of play for the mind. Visual puns are also a potent resource for the mind to correlate and cross-reference Artifacts, linking them together in suprising ways.

W E MUST ALWAYS endeavor to see the spiritual within the mundane. There is a kind of dream logic that must be apprehended; the way your mind represents concepts by using everyday objects and events to crystalize or reconstruct the essence of an idea. Consistency and internal logic are important in understanding the complex and interconnected network of symbols that comprise a dream. As most dream

We live within the dream of God, co-creating the world with our thoughts, words, and deeds. Therefore, dedicate each night's dreaming to Him. Walk in your dreams, as in your daily life, with the knowledge that your every action is shaping the world for yourself and for others. Dream responsibly and with compassionate action.

symbols point to something greater, the dreamer's task is to look beyond the icon to see the source.

A LIFETIME OF RESEARCH

BY SEEDING OUR DREAMS, we embark on a process of self-discovery that will enrich our lives and nurture our souls. Each new night brings with it the opportunity to recover lost treasures, explore new avenues for wisdom and knowledge, or enjoy the delights of emotional fulfillment. The experiences of our lives shape us like trees on a windswept hilltop, forming us into the image of our memories. As we rediscover the experiences of our dreaming selves, we reclaim some of the forces that have molded us.

IN OUR DREAMS, we may catch a glimpse of the blueprint which has guided the construction of our minds, and thus, gain some understanding of our spirit. We also may gain some small amount of control over the process of self-growth, so that we may have the possibility to gently guide both our dreams and our lives towards balance, knowledge, and harmony.

Dreams inevitably flow from the Creator, the ultimate source of generative energy. To seek illumination in your dreams means to follow the One Who Illumines. To find truth in your dreams you must discover the Source of Truth. To receive healing in your dreams you must first embrace the Great Healer.

May you dream with love, responsibility, gentleness, and hope, so that the fruit of your dreams will nurture not only yourself, but all of Creation.